The Collector's Series / Volume 17

Cooking With Honey

by Judy Powers

MORE GREAT RECIPES!

This book is just one of many cookbooks from our Collector's Series. These celebrated books make great gifts for family and friends—and for yourself.

Apple Magic	Holiday Entertaining (Xmas)
Barbeque	Hooked on Seafood
Chicken On The Run	Keys to Successful Baking
Chocolate Quick Fix	Light Cuisine
Chocolate Truffles	Microwave Magic
Cookies!	Muffins & Cupcakes
Cooking With Honey	Pizza Pizzazz
Cooking With Old Bay®	Salads
Creole & Cajun	Southern Style
Cuisine of India	Strawberries
Easy & Elegant Hors d'Oeuvres	Super Soups
Fast & Fabulous Hors d'Oeuvres	Vegetable Magic
From a Chinese Kitchen	

Send for more information on these great cookbooks.
Send a self-addressed, stamped business-size envelope (#10) to:
The American Cooking Guild
6-F East Cedar Avenue, Gaithersburg, MD 20877

Copyright © 1984 by Judy Powers

All rights reserved. No part of this publication may be reproduced in any way, electronic or mechanical, without written permission of the publisher; except in the case of review purposes, where no more than five recipes may be reprinted for use in that review.

ISBN 0-942320-12-3

Published by: The American Cooking Guild
6-F East Cedar Avenue
Gaithersburg, MD 20877
(301) 963-0698

Table of Contents

What is Honey? 6
    Composition 6
    Flavor 7
Cooking With Honey 8
Home Remedies and Beauty Secrets 9

Meats
    Tropical Steak 12
    Barbecued Spareribs 13
    Baked Lamb Shoulder 13
    Steak and Honey Barbecue 14
    Rolled-Beef Roast 14
    Honey Glazed Short Ribs 15
    Chili 15
    Ham Steak 16
    Pork Chops Supreme 16
    Oriental Pork 17
    Savory Pork Chops 17
    Mandarin Pork Chops 18
    Teriyaki Pork Chops 18
    Char Siu 19
    Beef or Chicken Teriyaki Marinade 19
    Hot Dog Cookout with Honey Baked Beans 20
    Turkey with Rice 20
    Chicken Lesley 21
    Honey Curried Chicken 21
    Chicken with Peppers and Walnuts 22
    Honey Chicken 22
    Lesley's Barbecued Chicken 23
    Barbecued Chicken 23
    Hawaiian Gold Chicken 24
    Western Style Peking Duck 25

Vegetables
    Sweet Potato Balls 26
    Glazed Sweet Potatoes 27
    Sweet Potato Casserole 27
    Spicy Beets 28
    Beets with Honey 28
    Carrots and Honey 29
    Nell Morgan's Marinated Carrots 29

Vegetable Glaze 30
Onions in a Casserole 30
Belle Young's Corn Pie 31
Fresh Corn Saute 31
Honeyed Squash 32
Zucchini in a Skillet 32
Honey Baked Beans 33
Baked Beans 33

Salads & Salad Dressings
Great Cole Slaw 34
Honey Bee Ambrosia 35
Polynesian Pineapple 35
Honey French Dressing 36
Creamy French Dressing 36
Italian Dressing 37
Honey Dressing 37
Russian Dressing 38
Blue Cheese Dressing 38
Mae Sanders' Fruit Salad Dressing 38

Breads
Swedish Rye Bread 39
Whole Wheat Bread 40
Honey Bran Bread 41
White Bread....................................41
Date Nut Bread 42
Honey Cornbread 42
Cheese Bread...................................43
Honey French Toast 44
Waffles with Orange Sauce 44

Sauces
Zesty Sauce 45
Corn Relish 46
India Relish 46
Mild Honey Mustard 47
Good Sauce for Steak 47
Honey Lemon Jelly 48
Honey Orange Butter 48
Pancake and Waffle Sauce 48

Cakes, Pies & Cookies
Lemon Honey Cake 49
White Cake 50
Lou McClure Willimon's Poppy Seed Cake 50
Applesauce Cake 51
Bette Hitch's Holland Honey Cake 51
Honey Fruitcake 52
Chocolate Cake 53
Carrot-Coconut Honey Cake 54
Cream Cheese Frosting 54
Harvest Pumpkin Pie 55
Pecan Pie 55
Fudge Brownies 56
Footprint Cookies 56
Peanut Butter Cookies 57
Milk and Honey Cookies 57
Honey-Oatmeal Bars 58
Macadamia Honey Twist 58
Lebkuchen 59

Other Good Things
Baked Bananas in Honey-Lemon Sauce 60
Chocolate Almond Sauce 61
Chocolate Fudge Icing 61
Honey Ice Cream 62
Fruit Roll Ups 62
Bob Jennings Cream Cheese and Honey Crepes 63
Honey Taffey 63
Strawberry Smoothie 63
Honey Chocolate Sauce 64
Party Eggnog 64

What Is Honey?

Honey is produced from the nectar of flowers or from other sweet liquids that worker bees eat during each day's flying which is finally stored in the cells of the beehives. Actually there are more than 10,000 varieties of bees, but only 5 perform this act of honey storage. It has been calculated that to obtain one pound of honey, bees have to visit at least one million flowers. A honey bee lives four to six weeks and can collect only a teaspoonful of nectar. Since many thousands of bees are employed to collect nectar and others in the hive must fan it with their wings to solidify it into honey, about 150,000 bees are required to produce one pound of honey. The flying distances involved in accumulating the nectar for that one pound are equivalent to flying three times around the earth.

Composition:

The composition of honey varies according to environmental conditions: relative humidity, floral source, ripeness when extracted from the comb, methods used in processing and conditions of storage. There are hundreds of varities of honey in the United States alone, and if you consider the world, the varieties of honey number in the thousands.

The following chart, prepared by the American Honey Institute, shows the average chemical composition of honey:

Principal Components	Per Cent
Water	17.7
Levulose (fruit sugar)	40.5
Dextrose (grape sugar)	34.0
Sucrose (cane sugar)	1.9
Dextrins and Gums	1.5
Ash (silicon, oron, copper, manganese, chlorine, calcium, potassium, sodium, phosphorus, sulfur, aluminum, magnesium)	0.18
Total	95.78

This leaves an undetermined factor of 4.22 per cent. There are minute amounts of enzymes, minerals, yeasts, acids, and other trace elements. It should be noted that one teaspoon of extracted honey contains about 21 calories.

Levulose (also called *fructose*) is a type of sugar found in fruits.

Dextrose (also called *glucose*) is a type of sugar less sweet than cane sugar, occurring naturally in fruits and especially in grapes.

Sucrose is a crystalline sugar found in sugar cane and sugar beets.

Dextrin is a gummy substance which is an important factor in making honey easily digestible.

Flavor:

The floral source of honey determines its flavor and aroma. If bees gather nectar from orange blossoms, the honey will have the taste and aroma of oranges. If bees gather nectar from sage blossoms, the honey will have the taste and aroma of sage. If bees gather from many sources like a field of wildflowers, the flavor of the honey will be indeterminable, a mixture of many flavors.

The honeybee generally works on only one source at a time. A colony, however, may gather nectar from two or more sources before the surplus is extracted by the beekeeper, and produce a natural blend of two or more distinct flavors. As a rule, bees control the source, by returning to the same flower for nectar. If fields are covered with only one type of flowering plant, they would more likely than not gather from that one source. A few stray bees going into another field would not alter the overall flavor or content of the honey.

Hygroscopic properties of honey:

Honey is hygroscopic, which means it has the power to draw moisture out of the air or out of any moisture-bearing material—even a stone crock. This characteristic of honey makes it highly desirable in commercially baked cookies, cakes, and breads, which remain *naturally* fresh. They don't require artificial preservatives to keep them fresh.

Cooking With Honey

Here are some rules that must be followed when cooking with honey that can assure success and pleasure:

Rule 1. When baking, set your oven at 25°F less than the recipe calls for on a receipe that does not contain honey. Baked goods brown faster when flavored with honey, so by baking breads and muffins longer at a lower temperature you get good results. When cooking on top of the stove, turn the heat down and stir a little more often because dishes made with honey stick a little sooner and burn a little quicker.

Rule 2. Honey adds liquid to a recipe (about three tablespoons of extra fluid per cup of sweetening, or one-quarter cup per pound). There is a good "rule of thumb" when honey is substituted for sugar in a recipe: *you must reduce the amount of liquid by ¼ cup for each cup of honey used to replace a cup of sugar.*

Rule 3. Honey is slightly acid, so add a little baking soda (usually one-eighth to one-quarter teaspoonful per cup of sweetening) to most batters and doughs. This addition is unnecessary with yeast breads because the bread leavening thrives in the mildly acid environment of honey.

Rule 4. The sugar in a recipe can usually be replaced with an equal *weight* of honey—a rule that works out to about two-thirds of a cup of liquid honey to one cup of dry sugar. Honey is largely fructose and is therefore much sweeter than refined sugar.

These rules do not apply to the recipes in this book, as they are recipes especially written for honey use and the proportions have already been changed. It's fun to be creative and see how your own favorite recipes can be changed and enhanced with the use of honey instead of sugar.

Pure honey will granulate (crystallize) if it becomes too cool, or has been stored for a while. This does not alter the flavor or the content of honey, but many cooks think that their honey has "spoiled." This is a natural process of honey, and many countries prefer their honey in this granulated form. It is very simple to liquefy your honey if you prefer it in that state: place the opened jar of honey in a pan of warm water for a while and it will become liquid again, or place your jar of honey in a microwave oven for about 30 seconds. Before you do this, you might try the honey granulated. It's lovely.

The flavor of a particular honey will also make quite a difference in your recipe. In small amounts, honey heightens flavor without itself being distinguishable. In greater proportion, it quickly tends to dominate a mixture. Light colored honeys tend to have a less pronounced effect in flavor combinations, so they should be chosen when an unidentifiable sweetness is desired. Dark mellow honeys, such as buckwheat, contribute flavor and are excellent in spicy pastries. Occasionally honeys, such as eucalyptus, are so strongly flavored that they are not recommended for cooking. Appreciate them on toast or in tea. A dish in which honey disguises or obliterates the natural flavors of the other ingredients is a disappointment even to a confirmed honey-eater.

Honey is like wine. To an educated palate, one honey is as distinguishable from another as is a burgundy or a Riesling. Different nectars and different regions with different climates determine the differences in the flavors of honey. Sample different honeys. You will soon discover your favorite flavors and find that some honeys are better than others for substitutions in your favorite recipes.

Here is a list of some common honey types in approximate order of mild flavor to strong flavor:

1. Tupelo
2. Clover (Alfalfa)
3. Sage
4. Palmetto
5. Sunflower
6. Gallberry
7. Goldenrod
8. Poplar
9. Buckwheat

The following flavors are very distinctive and should probably not be used in cooking, but should be enjoyed for themselves:
1. Orange
2. Basswood
3. Sourwood

Home Remedies and Beauty Secrets

In olden times, man used honey for almost every illness of the body and mind. Honey was good for the stomach and intestinal disorders. It was used as a gentle laxative. Honey was also used as a sedative. Modern research has found that honey increases blood calcium and has the same effect as a glass of milk before bedtime. Honey is good for the skin. It's antibacterial properties make honey a good, natural remedy for open wounds, skin rashes, and burns. It was the base for many home remedies such as cough syrup, diarrhea cures and even a cure for bedwetting.

Here are a few recipes for home remedies that might cure and certainly won't harm:

Burn Cure

Mix one egg yolk, one tablespoon of honey and one tablespoon of olive oil. Spread onto surgical gauze and place on the burned area. When the dressing dries, repeat the treatment until the healing is complete. The pain should subside and disappear completely in a short time.

Diarrhea Cure

Mix one teaspoon of honey in eight ounces of barley water in a glass and drink. This will stop summer diarrhea.

Bedwetting Cure

Before the child goes to bed, make sure he has no liquid refreshment. Just before he goes to sleep, give him at least 3 or 4 teaspoons of honey.

Tranquilizer

Before going to bed, steep one cup of camomile tea, fresh or dry mint leaves, and one teaspoon of honey for three minutes.

Cough Syrup I

For a simple cough syrup, mix equal parts of honey and lemon juice and use as needed.

Cough Syrup II

Blend well ¼ cup glycerine and ¼ cup of honey and 1 tablespoon of fresh lime or lemon juice. Keep in a tightly-covered jar and take one teaspoon every two hours, or as needed.

Cough Syrup III

Mix equal parts of honey, bourbon whiskey, and lemon juice for a truly exceptional cough syrup. Take as needed.

Tonic

Two teaspoons of honey and two teaspoons of apple cider vinegar taken in a glass of water one or more times daily, will replenish the body's minerals. Take as needed when doing mental or physical work.

You might enjoy these beauty secrets. Some date back to the time of Cleopatra!

Honey Facial

Starting with a perfectly clean face, pat on enough honey to cover. Lie down for 30 minutes and relax. Clean the face with warm water and a clean washcloth. If your face is oily, add a little apple cider vinegar or lemon juice to the rinse water.

Oatmeal Facial

Mix ⅓ cup of finely ground oatmeal with enough honey (two or three teaspoons) to make a smooth paste. Spread the mixture over the face but not around the eyes and let it remain for 30 minutes. Rinse face and pat dry.

Facial for Acne

Mix ⅓ cup of honey with ⅔ cups of water. Pat gently all over the face or affected areas. Let this mixture remain for 20 or 30 minutes, rinse well and pat dry.

For Dry Skin

Mix 1 tablespoon of sweet almond oil with 2 tablespoons of honey. Blend and spread over a clean face and neck and allow to remain for 15 minutes or more. Rinse face with lukewarm water and pat dry.

For Oily Skin

Mix 1 tablespoon of honey, 1 tablespoon of lemon juice, and 2-3 drops of milk. Mix into a smooth paste and spread over face and neck. Allow to remain for 10 to 15 minutes and rinse with lukewarm water and pat dry. Do not use more than once every 2 weeks or once a month if your skin dries up too much.

Honey Hand Scrub

Mix three tablespoons finely ground cornmeal, two tablespoons of honey and one tablespoon of cornstarch in a small, unbreakable container. Leave near the sink and use as you would any hand soap. It softens, cleans and soothes the hands, and should always be rinsed with cold water.

Hand Cream

- 8 egg yolks
- 2 cups honey
- 2 cups almond oil
- ½ pound bitter almonds, finely minced
- ½ teaspoon oil of orange

Beat egg yolks with honey, add almond oil gradually, and then almonds and oil of orange. Apply small amount to hands to maintain a youthful appearance.

Meats

Tropical Steak

```
3      pounds round steak
1      teaspoon salt
2      Tablespoons salad oil or drippings
1      large onion
1½     cups chopped celery
1      medium green pepper, seeded and diced
1      can (1 pound 4½ ounces) pineapple chunks
1      fresh tomato, peeled, seeded and cubed
1      Tablespoon corn starch
¼      cup honey
1      Tablespoon soy sauce or Worcestershire
```

Cut meat in cubes; sprinkle with salt. Brown in oil; remove meat; set aside. In same skillet, saute onion, celery, and green pepper about 5 minutes. Drain pineapple; reserve ½ cup liquid. Add pineapple chunks and tomato to vegetables.

Moisten corn starch with pineapple juice; add honey and soy sauce. Blend into vegetables, add meat. Cover and cook at 325° (slow) 2 hours or until tender. Stir occasionally to blend and prevent sticking.

Makes 6 servings.

Barbecued Spareribs

¼ cup oil
1 large onion, chopped fine
1 6-ounce can tomato paste
¼ cup vinegar
½ cup water
¼ cup honey
½ cup Worcestershire sauce
1 teaspoon salt
1 teaspoon thyme
⅛ teaspoon garlic powder
1 teaspoon dry mustard
4 pounds spareribs

Heat oil in a large skillet, add onion and stir 3 to 4 minutes without allowing onion to brown. Mix tomato paste and vinegar and add to skillet, stir in all other ingredients except beef, and simmer uncovered for 10 to 15 minutes. Place ribs, fat side up, on a rack in a 400° oven. Brush meat with sauce, and bake for 45 minutes to 1 hour or until tender, basting every 10 to 15 minutes. Meat should be crisp and brown. Cut into portions and serve at once.
Serves 4 to 6.

Baked Lamb Shoulder

5-6 pounds shoulder of lamb
½ cup honey
½ cup lemon juice
    salt
    garlic powder
    dried, crushed mint leaves

Marinate meat in combined honey, juice, salt and garlic powder, turning to coat and refrigerate overnight or for several hours. Turn occasionally. Drain meat, reserving marinade.

Place in roasting pan. Score meat, salt to taste. Roast, uncovered, in a 325° oven about 40 minutes to the pound, basting frequently with marinade. When half done, sprinkle on mint leaves, and continue roasting.
Serves 8.

Steak and Honey Barbecue

1 steak per person, scored
2 Tablespoons crushed red peppers
1 teaspoon salt
1 thinly sliced onion
½ cup honey

Marinate steak in the mixture of crushed red peppers, salt, sliced onions, and honey. Grill to desired doneness. This marinade will cover 2 large or 4 small steaks.

Rolled-Beef Roast

5 Tablespoons oil
4-5 pounds rolled rump roast
1 teaspoon seasoned salt
⅛ teaspoon garlic powder
¼ cup soy sauce
¾ cup water
1½ Tablespoons honey
1 Tablespoon vinegar
½ teaspoon ginger
2½ Tablespoons corn starch

In heavy kettle, heat oil and brown meat on all sides, sprinkle with seasoned salt mixed with garlic powder. Mix half the soy sauce with water, add honey, vinegar, and ginger, and pour over meat. Cover. Simmer gently about 3 hours or until very tender, turning meat about every 30 minutes, and adding water if necessary.

When done, lift the meat from the pan, cut the strings, and keep warm while making gravy. Skim fat from juices. Mix remainder of soy sauce with corn starch, add to pan juices, and cook until thickened, stirring constantly.

Serves 8.

Oriental Pork

1	pound pork, sliced thin
5	Tablespoons oil
2½	green peppers, seeded and sliced
1	large can water chestnuts, drained and diced
1	16-ounce can pineapple tidbits, drained
1	cup water
2	Tablespoons corn starch
3	Tablespoons honey
4	Tablespoons soy sauce
½	cup water

Brown the pork in heated oil. Add peppers and sauté briefly. Add water chestnuts, pineapple, and 1 cup water, and bring to a boil. Mix remaining ingredients together, then stir into the pork. Simmer, stirring, until mixture is thick and clear.
Serves 8.

Savory Pork Chops

6	pork chops (½ inch thick)
⅓	cup honey
¾	cup chili sauce or catsup
2	Tablespoons water
6	thin onion slices
6	thin lemon slices

In small bowl, mix together honey, chili sauce and water. Spread half of mixture over bottom of shallow baking pan. Place chops over marinade. Spoon balance of marinade over chops. Cover each chop with a slice of onion and lemon. Bake at 325° for 45 minutes, baste with sauce, continue baking until chops are fork tender (about 1 hour).

Mandarin Pork Chops

    2   pork tenderloins or 8 thick pork chops
    ½   cup oil
    ⅛   teaspoon garlic powder or 1 garlic clove, minced
    3   tablespoons honey
    1   Tablespoon ginger
    1   Tablespoon dry mustard
    1   cup soy sauce

Place the meat in a shallow pan. Combine the oil, garlic, honey, spices, and soy sauce for a marinade, and pour over meat. Refrigerate, turning occasionally, for 24 hours. Remove from marinade and grill over coals for about 35 minutes, or until well done, turning the meat as it browns.
Serves 8.

Teriyaki Pork Chops

    6-8   pork chops
    ½   cup wine vinegar (red or white)
    ¼   cup soy sauce
    ½   cup honey
    1   clove garlic, minced
    ½   teaspoon ground ginger
    1   cup canned crushed pineapple (juice and all)
    1   Tablespoon corn starch

Trim most of the fat from pork chops and arrange in shallow baking dish overlapping chops if necessary. Cover with foil and bake at 350° for 45 minutes.

Combine all remaining ingredients in a small saucepan and heat, stirring constantly, until thickened. Pour sauce over pork chops and continue baking, uncovered, until tender, about 30 minutes longer. Especially nice with steamed rice and a tropical fruit salad.

Char Siu

1½	pounds boneless pork, cut into chunks
3	tablespoons brown sugar
½	teaspoon salt
1	teaspoon honey
1	teaspoon soy sauce
1	Tablespoon white wine
3	Tablespoons red bean curd sauce (nam yue)
1	Tablespoon red food coloring (optional)
⅓	cup water
⅛	teaspoon five-spice powder
	paper clips for roasting

Rub sugar on chunks of pork. Let stand 5 minutes. Combine all remaining ingredients but paper clips. Pour over pork, marinate all night in refrigerator.

To roast pork, preheat oven to 350°F. Invert paperclips so they form the letter S. Place a rack at top of oven and another rack at bottom of oven. Place a large sheet-cake baking pan with water on bottom rack. Hook each piece of pork on a paper clip and hang pork from top shelf. Roast pork for 1 hour, occasionally basting with marinade.

Beef or Chicken Teriyaki Marinade

1-1½"	ginger root peeled and grated or pressed
1½	Tablespoons honey
2	cloves garlic, pressed
½	cup soy sauce

Combine above ingredients to make marinade.

Marinate chicken pieces or steak for two or more hours in refrigerator. Delicious baked, broiled or barbecued.

Hot Dog Cookout with Honey Baked Beans

  2   Tablespoons shortening
  1   Tablespoon soy sauce
  1   teaspoon prepared mustard
½   cup honey
  1   Tablespoon vinegar
  1   teaspoon corn starch
  1   package hot dogs
  1   package hamburger buns
       Honey Baked Beans, see recipe, page 33

Mix first six ingredients together in a saucepan and simmer 8-10 minutes, until sauce becomes smooth and thick. Cut each hot dog halfway through in several places along one side only. Place on cookie sheet. Baste with sauce several times while grilling. (When cooking, hot dogs on grill will form a circle.) Place rounded hot dogs on toasted hamburger buns and fill with baked beans.

Turkey with Rice

   6   cups cooked, diced turkey
  ¾   cup honey
   6   Tablespoons prepared mustard
        salt
1½   teaspoons curry powder
   6   Tablespoons turkey drippings
   3   cups cooked rice

Mix honey, mustard, salt, curry powder, and drippings thoroughly. (A little cayenne pepper may be added if you like it "hot.") Combine lightly with diced turkey and heat, stirring lightly. Serve over hot, cooked rice.
Serves 8.

Chicken Lesley

    flour
    salt and pepper
¼ *cup soy sauce*
¼ *cup honey*
¼ *cup lemon juice*
¼ *cup butter*
1 *chicken or 2 whole chicken breasts or 4 Cornish hens*

Lightly dredge chicken or hens in flour, pepper and salt. Bake at 325° chicken or hens. for 1 hour. Mix soy sauce, honey, lemon juice and butter; baste with sauce every 20 minutes for an additional 45 minutes. The chicken will be golden brown and crispy.
Serves 4 to 6.

Honey Curried Chicken

1 *2½-3 pound fryer chicken, cut up*
¼ *cup butter, melted*
½ *cup honey*
¼ *cup prepared mustard*
1 *teaspoon salt*
½ *teaspoon curry powder (or more)*

Wash and dry chicken. Combine remaining ingredients, stirring well. Dip each piece of chicken into the resulting sauce, coating well. Reserve remaining sauce. Place chicken, skin side up, in roasting pan. Bake at 375° for 1 hour, basting occasionally with sauce.
Serves 4 to 5.

Chicken with Peppers and Walnuts

1½	pounds boned chicken breasts, skinned
3	Tablespoons soy sauce
2	teaspoons corn starch
2	Tablespoons dry sherry
½	teaspoon salt
¼	teaspoon ground ginger
¼	teaspoon crushed red pepper
1	teaspoon honey
2	Tablespoons peanut oil
1	cup walnut halves
1	clove garlic, finely minced
2	medium green peppers, seeded and cut into strips
5	green onions (tops and bottoms) bias-sliced into 1-inch lengths

Cut chicken into 1-inch pieces. Set aside. In small bowl blend soy sauce into corn starch; stir in sherry, salt, ginger, red pepper and honey. Set aside.

Preheat wok to 375°; add oil. Stir-fry walnuts 1 to 2 minutes or till just golden. Remove from wok. Add chicken and garlic to *hot* wok; stir 2-3 minutes. Push chicken up sides (remove if using skillet); add peppers and onions and stir-fry 2 minutes or till tender-crisp.

Stir soy mixture; add to chicken and peppers. Cook and stir till thickened and bubbly; cover and cook 1 minute more. Add walnuts and serve at once.

Serves 4 to 5.

Honey Chicken

2½-3	pounds chicken pieces
2	Tablespoons cooking oil
½	cup melted butter
¼	cup lemon juice
½	cup honey
1	teaspoon ground ginger

Brown chicken quickly on all sides in melted butter and oil in heavy skillet. Combine remaining ingredients and pour over browned chicken. Cover and cook over low heat 30-40 minutes until chicken is tender. Baste occasionally.

Serves 4 to 6.

Lesley's Barbecued Chicken

- 1 whole chicken cut in quarters
- 1 14½-ounce can stewed tomatoes
- 1 medium Spanish onion, chopped
- 2 stalks of celery, chopped fine
- juice of 1 lemon
- ½ cup honey (or more)
- 4 Tablespoons Worcestershire sauce
- salt and pepper to taste
- 1 teaspoon tabasco sauce

Mix together all the ingredients except the chicken in saucepan and heat to blend. Place chicken, breast side down in a shallow baking dish, and pour half the sauce over chicken. Bake for 45 minutes at 325°. Turn chicken over, and pour rest of sauce over and bake another 45 minutes until chicken is tender and brown. This is also good for thick pork chops.
Serves 4 to 6.

Barbecued Chicken

- ½ cup corn oil
- 1 cup lemon juice
- 2 Tablespoons honey
- 2 teaspoons salt
- 1 teaspoon hot pepper sauce
- 3 whole broiler-fryer chicken breasts, halved

In saucepan, stir together the first five ingredients. Bring to boil over medium heat. Place chicken on grill, skin side up, about 8 inches from source of heat. Baste chicken with sauce and cook, turning and basting often, 45 minutes or until chicken is fork-tender.
Makes 6 servings.

Hawaiian Gold Chicken

This recipe is featured on the cover using the cornish hen variation.

1 fryer chicken, about 3-3½ pounds
4 Tablespoons butter
½ cup honey
2 teaspoons fine herbs (tarragon, rosemary, basil, etc.)
2 Tablespoons Dijon style mustard
½ teaspoon garlic salt
¼ cup dry white wine
½ teaspoon pepper (white or black)

Remove giblets from chicken, rinse with cold water and pat dry. Melt butter over low heat and add honey, herbs, mustard, garlic salt, wine, and pepper. Bring to a boil, stirring. Remove from heat. Brush inner and outer surfaces of chicken with marinade.

Roast, loosely tented with aluminum foil, in 375° oven for 1 hour. Remove tent and continue roasting uncovered, basting occasionally with marinade, for an additional 30-45 minutes or until skin is a beautiful brown and juices run clear when thigh is pricked with fork.

Skim fat from drippings and combine them with remaining marinade. Pour sauce over quartered chicken servings.

Serves 4.

VARIATION: Substitute 2 cornish hens for the fryer chicken. Reduce the temperature to 350° and cut roasting time by 15-20 minutes.

NOTE: This may also be made in a clay pot. Pour marinade over chicken; bake at 450° until done—about 1 hour. Skim fat from drippings.

Western Style Peking Duck

2 ducks, each 4½ to 5 pounds
1 teaspoon each ground ginger and ground cinnamon
½ teaspoon each ground nutmeg and ground white pepper
¼ teaspoon ground cloves
2 Tablespoons soy sauce
1 Tablespoon honey
8 green onions, cut in thin slices (include some of the tops)
½-1 cup canned Chinese plum sauce
chopped parsley

Rinse ducks inside and out and pat dry; reserve giblets for other uses. Blend the ginger, cinnamon, nutmeg, pepper and cloves. Dust ½ teaspoon of the spice mixture inside each duck and then rub the remaining spices evenly over the exterior of the birds. Close the abdominal cavity with small skewers. Wrap each duck separately in foil, folding the edges to seal tightly. You can do this ahead and chill.

Place ducks side by side in a large pan and bake in a 425° oven for 1 hour. Remove and let stand about 15 minutes, or until slightly cooled. Then carefully open foil at one end and drain out accumulated juices and fat (the juices are good added to seasoned broth to make soup for another meal). Discard the foil.

Set ducks slightly apart on a rack in the baking pan and prick skin lightly all over with a fork. Bake at 375° for 30 minutes. Blend soy sauce with honey and brush onto ducks. Return ducks to oven and raise temperature to 500°. Bake about 5 minutes or until very richly browned; take care not to char.

Cut ducks in halves with kitchen scissors or poultry shears. Put a half on each serving plate and garnish with parsley. Set out the green onions, plum sauce, and chopped parsley in separate bowls or individual servings.

Vegetables

Sweet Potato Balls

2½ cups mashed sweet potatoes
¾ teaspoon salt
   dash black pepper
2 Tablespoons melted butter
¼ cup miniature marshmallows
1 Tablespoon butter
⅓ cup honey
1 cup chopped pecans

    Combine mashed sweet potatoes, salt, pepper and 2 tablespoons melted butter. Stir in marshmallows. Chill mixture in refrigerator for easier handling. Shape into balls, using ¼ cup mashed potato mixture for each ball. Heat one tablespoon butter and ⅓ cup of honey in small heavy skillet. When syrup is hot add potato balls one at a time.
    Carefully (with two forks) roll each ball in syrup for quick glaze. Lift out of syrup and roll in chopped nuts. Place on greased or foil-lined baking pan. Be sure they do not touch! Bake in 350° oven for 15 to 20 minutes.
    Makes 10 balls.

Glazed Sweet Potatoes

    5-6   sweet potatoes, boiled
    ½   cup honey
    ½   cup orange juice
    ⅓   cup butter
    1   teaspoon salt

Arrange peeled, sliced potatoes in greased casserole, spooning the combined remaining ingredients between layers. Bake at 375^0 about 30 minutes, basting frequently. May also be cooked in heavy skillet on top of range.
Serves 8.

Sweet Potato Casserole

    2   eggs
    ¼   cup melted butter
    ½   cup honey
    1   teaspoon lemon juice
    ½   teaspoon grated lemon rind
    1   cup evaporated milk
         salt to taste
    1   Tablespoon vanilla
    ½   teaspoon nutmeg
    1   teaspoon ginger
    2   cups grated raw sweet potatoes

Beat eggs with honey until light. Add melted butter, lemon juice, lemon rind, evaporated milk, salt, vanilla, nutmeg and ginger, adding sweet potatoes last. Mix well and put into buttered casserole dish. Bake at 250^0 for 45 minutes. Halfway through the baking process, stir mixture once.

Spicy Beets

1	1-pound can diced beets, drained
3⅓	Tablespoons margarine or butter
2½	Tablespoons honey
2	Tablespoons prepared mustard
1¼	teaspoons Worcestershire sauce
	salt to taste

Combine all ingredients except beets, and simmer over low heat until smooth. Add beets and heat. May be heated on top of stove or put into a 350° oven for 10 to 15 minutes.
Serves 4.

Beets with Honey

2	cups diced or sliced beets, cooked or canned
1	Tablespoon corn starch
½	teaspoon salt
1	Tablespoon water or beet juice
¼	cup honey
1	Tablespoon butter or margarine
2	Tablespoons vinegar

Heat beets, drain. Mix corn starch and salt, blend in water. Add honey, butter and vinegar. Cook over low heat, stirring constantly until thick. Add sauce to beets, and let stand ten minutes to absorb flavors. Reheat.
Serves 4 to 6.

Carrots and Honey

    5-6   carrots, peeled and cut into ½-inch slices
    ¼   cup margarine or butter
    ½   cup honey
    2-3   Tablespoons chopped parsley
          salt and pepper to taste

Drop the carrots in boiling salted water, cook until tender, (about 10 minutes), drain. Melt margarine and add remaining ingredients, blending well. Heat carrots in sauce and serve. Or cooked carrots may be put into a greased casserole, the sauce poured over, and baked covered in a 350° oven 20 to 30 minutes. Variation: ¼ cup of prepared mustard may be added to sauce if desired.
Serves 8.

Nell Morgan's Marinated Carrots

    1   pound carrots, sliced
    1   can tomato soup
    ¼   cup honey
    ½   cup vinegar
    ½   cup light oil
    1   green pepper, chopped
    1   large onion, chopped

Slice the carrots and cook briefly in salted water. Mix together the honey, vinegar, and oil with tomato soup and heat. Mix with slightly cooked carrots and add chopped onions and peppers and marinate overnight. This goes well with smoked salmon.

Vegetable Glaze

¼   cup honey
2   Tablespoons sugar
1   Tablespoon butter
1   Tablespoon lemon juice
1   Tablespoon Worcestershire sauce
1   teaspoon vinegar
¼   teaspoon salt
⅛   teaspoon pepper
3-4 cups cooked vegetables

Combine all ingredients except vegetables in a skillet. Stir and let boil for one minute. Add vegetables and simmer until heated through.

Onions in a Casserole

3   cups small pearl onions
⅓   cup honey
½   cup catsup
1½ Tablespoons butter or margarine
     salt to taste

Cook onions in salted water ten minutes. Drain and put them in a baking dish. Mix honey, catsup, and butter and pour over. Cover and bake about an hour in 350° oven, basting occasionally. Uncover for last 15 to 20 minutes if too juicy.
   VARIATION: omit catsup and add a little sherry and slivered almonds.
   Serves 6.

Belle Young's Corn Pie

2   14½-ounce cans creamed corn
4   eggs
2   cups milk
1-2   Tablespoon(s) flour
1½   Tablespoons honey

Butter a casserole dish. Mix all ingredients and bake in a 325° oven until it sets (test with knife).

Fresh Corn Sauté

3   Tablespoons butter
1   onion, chopped
1   green pepper, diced
4   cups fresh corn kernels, cut from cob
¼   cup water
1   Tablespoon honey
1   teaspoon salt
    freshly ground pepper
2   Tablespoons chopped pimiento
½   cup grated cheese or crumbled, cooked bacon

Melt butter in a medium skillet with cover. Saute onion and green pepper until tender. Add corn, water, honey, seasonings, and pimiento. Cover and cook over low heat stirring several times until corn is tender-crisp. Serve hot with cheese or bacon.
Serves 6.

Honeyed Squash

3	acorn or Hubbard squash
½	cup honey
½	cup butter, melted
½	teaspoon salt
⅓	teaspoon cinnamon
¼	teaspoon ginger

Cut squash in half, remove seeds and fiber. Put in shallow baking pan, cut side down, add ½ of water, and bake 30 minutes in 375° oven. Turn squash upright, and drain liquid. Combine remaining ingredients and pour into squash hollows. Bake 15 minutes or until tender, basting frequently with sauce.
Serves 6.

Zucchini in a Skillet

4	medium zucchini
¼	cup mild-flavored honey (clover)
2	Tablespoons water
1	teaspoon butter or margarine
1	teaspoon dry French salad dressing mix
1	large tomato, cut in eighths

Wash zucchini, cut off ends. Cut in quarters lengthwise. In skillet, combine honey, water, butter and salad dressing mix. Arrange zucchini, cut side down, in honey mixture. Bring to boil, reduce heat and simmer about 20 minutes or until tender. Add tomato wedges and cook several minutes longer, turning once.
  Variation: Use broccoli, carrots, celery, parsnips, or squash in place of zucchini.
Makes 4 servings.

Honey Baked Beans

- ¼ cup fat or salad oil
- 2 cups chopped onion
- 1 pound ground beef
- 1 teaspoon salt
- 1 cup tomato catsup
- 2 Tablespoons prepared mustard
- 2 teaspoons cider vinegar
- ½ cup honey
- 2 16-ounce cans pork and beans
- 1 can kidney beans, drained

Heat fat in skillet. Add onions, simmer until golden yellow. Add ground beef. Stir with fork while onions brown slightly. Add remaining ingredients. Pour into bean pot or a 2-quart casserole. Bake in hot oven (400°) for 30 minutes.
Makes 8 servings.

Baked Beans

- ½ cup coarsely chopped onion
- 1 medium green pepper, diced
- 1 clove garlic, finely chopped
- 2 Tablespoons butter
- 2 cans (1 pound 12 oz.) baked beans, undrained
- ½ cup hot or seasoned catsup
- ¼ cup honey
- 1 cup grated sharp cheese
- ½ cup dry bread crumbs
- salt, pepper, paprika

Sauté onion, green pepper and garlic in butter until tender. Remove from heat; mix with beans, catsup and honey. Pour into 2 quart casserole. Combine cheese, crumbs, and seasonings; spoon over bean mixture. Bake uncovered at 350° until mixture is hot and top is browned (about 45 minutes). Freezes well (freeze before adding topping).
Makes 8 servings.

Salads & Salad Dressings

Great Cole Slaw

    1   cup honey
    1   cup cider or white wine vinegar
    ½   cup finely chopped onion
    1   teaspoon salt
    1   teaspoon celery seed (optional)
    1   large head cabbage (about 4 cups), finely chopped
    1   cup diced green pepper
    1   cup diced celery

    Combine honey with vinegar, onion, salt and celery seed in a small saucepan. Bring to boil; reduce heat and simmer 5 minutes. Cool. Pour cooled dressing over prepared vegetables and toss lightly. Cover and chill overnight to blend flavors.
    Makes 10-12 servings.

Honey Bee Ambrosia

    4   medium oranges, peeled and sliced crosswise
    3   bananas, sliced
    ½   cup orange juice
    ¼   cup honey
    2   Tablespoons lemon juice
    ¼   cup flaked coconut
         maraschino cherry halves (optional)

    Combine sliced fruit in a medium bowl, toss lightly. Combine orange juice, honey and lemon juice; pour over fruit and mix well. Sprinkle with coconut, cover and chill at least 1 hour. Garnish fruit with maraschino cherries, if desired.
Serves 6.

Polynesian Pineapple

    1   cup mayonnaise
    1   Tablespoon honey
    2   teaspoons prepared mustard
    2   small pineapples, halved lengthwise
    1   17-ounce can apricot halves, drained, halved
    2   cups diced cooked ham
    ⅓   cup raisins
    ½   cup slivered blanched almonds, toasted

    Stir together first 3 ingredients: set aside. Hollow out pineapple halves leaving ½ shell intact. Remove core; cut pineapple into chunks. In large bowl toss together pineapple, apricots, ham, raisins, ¼ cup of almonds, and dressing. Spoon into pineapple halves and garnish with remaining almonds. Serve immediately.
Makes 4 servings.
    Note: One 20-ounce can pineapple chunks, drained, may be substituted for fresh pineapple.

Honey French Dressing

⅓ cup honey
⅓ cup oil
⅓ cup vinegar
⅓ cup catsup
½ teaspoon salt
½ teaspoon pepper
½ teaspoon celery seed
½ teaspoon paprika

Combine all ingredients in blender until well blended. Serve over mixed greens or fruit.

Creamy French Dressing

1 cup mayonnaise
2 Tablespoons lemon juice
1 Tablespoon honey
1 Tablespoon milk
1 teaspoon paprika
½ teaspoon dry mustard
¼ teaspoon salt
⅛ teaspoon pepper

Stir together all ingredients; cover and chill.
Makes 1¼ cups.

Italian Dressing

1	cup mayonnaise
3	Tablespoons milk
1	Tablespoon cider vinegar
1	clove garlic, minced
½	teaspoon dried oregano leaves
¼	teaspoon honey
¼	teaspoon salt
⅛	teaspoon pepper

Stir together all ingredients. Cover. Chill.
Makes 1½ cups.

Honey Dressing

⅔	cups sugar
2	teaspoons salt
½	cup lemon juice
⅔	cup honey
2	teaspoons dry mustard
1¼	cup oil
¼	teaspoon paprika

Put all ingredients in a blender and blend a few minutes. Refrigerate. Delicious on fresh fruits. Add 1 teaspoon of celery seed over the salad.

Russian Dressing

    1   cup mayonnaise
    ⅓   cup catsup
    ⅓   cup chopped dill pickles
    2   teaspoons lemon juice
    2   teaspoons honey

Stir together all ingredients. Cover, chill.
Makes 1½ cups.

Blue Cheese Dressing

    1   cup mayonnaise
    4   ounces blue cheese, crumbled
    3   Tablespoons milk
    2   Tablespoons lemon juice
    1   Tablespoon finely chopped onion
    2   teaspoons honey
    ¼   teaspoon salt
    ¼   teaspoon dry mustard
    ¼   teaspoon Worcestershire sauce

Stir together all ingredients. Cover, chill.
Makes about 1½ cups.

Mae Sanders' Fruit Salad Dressing

    ⅓   cup crunchy peanut butter
    ⅓   cup mayonnaise
    ⅓   cup clover honey

Put all ingredients in blender and mix.
Makes 1 cup.

Breads

Swedish Rye Bread

- ⅓ cup honey
- ⅓ cup light molasses
- 2 cups warm water
- 2 packages dry yeast
- ⅓ cup vegetable oil
- 1½ teaspoons salt
- 2 cups rye flour
- 5-6 cups white flour
- grated orange peel or cardamon seed, if desired

Measure honey and molasses in mixing bowl, then add water and yeast. Let yeast dissolve. Add half of flour and mix well. Add salt, oil, flavoring and then rest of flour, gradually. Knead about ten minutes. If using a bread mixer, follow directions of mixer. Works well mixing with mixer or by hand.

Let dough rise until doubled in bulk. Knead down, cover and let stand 15 minutes. Shape into loaves or rolls and let double in bulk again. Bake in 375° oven for 45 minutes.

You may want to cover with foil the last part of baking to prevent overbrowning.

Note: For a darker bread, use blackstrap molasses.

Makes three large 9x5x3-inch loaves.

Whole Wheat Bread

½	cup honey
2¼	cups warm water
2	packages dry yeast
1	teaspoon salt
½	cup powdered milk
¼	cup vegetable oil
3	cups whole wheat flour
5-6	cups white flour

   Measure honey in a mixing bowl, then add water and yeast. Let yeast dissolve. Add half flour and mix well. Add salt, oil, powdered milk and then rest of flour, gradually. Knead about ten minutes. If using bread mixer, follow directions of mixer. Works well mixing with mixer or by hand.
   Let dough rise until doubled in bulk. Knead down, cover and let stand 15 minutes. Shape into loaves or rolls and let double in bulk again. Bake at 375° for 45 minutes.
   You may want to cover with foil the last part of baking to prevent overbrowning.
   Makes two large 9x5x3 loaves.

Honey Bran Bread

1	cup honey
¼	cup bran
1	cup whole-wheat flour
1	teaspoon double-acting baking powder
½	teaspoon salt
½	teaspoon baking soda
1	egg
¾	cup plus 2 tablespoons sour milk
1	cup raisins

Combine bran, whole-wheat flour, baking powder, salt, and soda. Combine and beat egg, sour milk and honey. Beat dry ingredients into liquid ingredients and add raisins. Place batter in 2 buttered 8x4-inch loaf pans. Allow to stand for 1 hour.

Bake in moderate oven (375º) for 1 hour or more. Serve very lightly toasted, with butter or honey and butter mixed.
Makes two loaves.

White Bread

3	Tablespoons honey
2	cups warm water
1	package dry yeast
¼	cup dry milk
3	Tablespoons vegetable oil
1¼	teaspoons salt
5-6	cups white flour

Measure honey in mixing bowl before water, then water and yeast. Let yeast dissolve. Add half of the flour and mix well. Add salt, oil and dry milk, then rest of flour, gradually. Knead about ten minutes. If using bread mixer, follow directions of mixer. Works well mixing with mixer or by hand.

Let dough rise until doubled in bulk. Knead down, cover and let stand 15 minutes. Shape into loaves or rolls. Let dough double in bulk again and then bake in a 400º oven for 30 minutes.

You may want to cover with foil the last part of baking to prevent overbrowning.
Makes two large 9x5x3-inch loaves.

Date Nut Bread

½	pound (1½ cups) dates, chopped fine
3	Tablespoons margarine or butter
½	cup sugar
½	cup honey
1	cup boiling water
3	cups sifted flour
½	teaspoon salt
1½	teaspoons baking powder
1½	teaspoons soda
1	egg, slightly beaten
1	cup chopped nuts

Combine first five ingredients and let cool. Sift dry ingredients. Add egg to date mixture. Stir into dry ingredients; add nuts. Bake in well greased and floured 9x5x3-inch loaf pan at 350° for 50 to 60 minutes or until done. Cool thoroughly.
Makes one loaf.

Honey Cornbread

2½	cups yellow cornmeal
1	cup whole wheat flour
2½	teaspoons baking powder
1	teaspoon baking soda
1	teaspoon salt
2½	cups buttermilk
½	cup vegetable oil
2	eggs, beaten
2	Tablespoons honey

Combine dry ingredients in large mixing bowl. Add remaining ingredients and mix well. Pour batter into greased 13x9-inch pan. Bake at 425° for 20-25 minutes or until golden brown.
Makes about 2 dozen 2-inch squares.

Cheese Bread

1	cup milk
¼	cup honey
1	Tablespoon seasoned salt
2	packages active dry yeasts or 2 yeast cakes
½	cup warm water
¼	pound (1 cup) sharp Cheddar cheese, grated
1	teaspoon dry mustard
⅛	teaspoon cayenne pepper
4½-5	cups sifted flour

In a small saucepan, heat milk just until bubbles form around edge of pan. Remove from heat. Add honey and seasoned salt, stirring until dissolved. Cool to lukewarm.

Sprinkle yeast over warm water in large bowl, stirring until dissolved. Stir in milk mixture, cheese, mustard, cayenne pepper and 2 cups of flour. Beat with wooden spoon until smooth, about 2 minutes. Gradually add remaining flour; mix in last of it by hand until dough leaves sides of bowl.

Turn dough onto lightly floured board. Grease fingers before kneading until dough is smooth, about 10 minutes. Place in lightly greased large bowl, turn once to bring greased side up and cover with towel. Let rise in warm place (85°) free from drafts, until double in size, about 2 hours.

Punch down dough, turn onto lightly floured board, shape into loaf. Place in greased 9x5x3-inch loaf pan. Cover loaf with towel, let rise until double, about 1 hour.

Bake at 400° for 30 to 35 minutes. Cover with aluminum foil for the last 10 to 15 minutes of baking. Turn out of pan and cool on rack.

Makes one loaf.

Honey French Toast

    2   eggs, slightly beaten
    ¼   cup milk
    ¼   cup honey
    ¼   teaspoon salt
    8   slices bread
         butter for frying
    1   cup honey
    2   Tablespoons lemon juice
    2   Tablespoons butter

Combine beaten eggs, ¼ cup milk, ¼ cup honey, and salt; dip bread in mixture and fry in butter until golden brown. Combine 1 cup honey, lemon juice, and 2 Tablespoons butter, heat. Serve over toast.
Serves 2 to 4.

Waffles with Orange Sauce

    3   eggs
    2   Tablespoons honey
    2   Tablespoons butter, melted
1⅓   cups milk
    2   cups biscuit mix

         Sauce:
1½   cups orange juice
 ½   cup honey
 ⅓   cup chopped nuts or dates

Beat eggs with honey, mixing thoroughly. Blend in butter and milk. Add biscuit mix and mix until smooth. Bake in preheated waffle iron; keep warm in oven. Make sauce: combine orange juice, honey, and nuts or dates; simmer 5 minutes. Serve hot over waffles.
Makes 4 waffles and 2 cups sauce.

Sauces

Zesty Sauce

Peps up beef, chicken or shrimp

1 can (15-ounces) or 2 cans (8-ounces) tomato sauce with tomato bits
2 Tablespoons honey
2 Tablespoons wine or cider vinegar
1 clove garlic, minced
2 green onions finely chopped (with tops)
2 Tablespoons diced canned green chillies
   few drops of red pepper sauce

Combine all ingredients. Over low heat stir and cook 5 minutes, or until onion is soft. May be used as a sauce over ground beef patties.
Makes about 2 cups.

Corn Relish

12	ears sweet corn
8	green peppers
4	red peppers
12	ripe tomatoes
1	quart onions
5	Tablespoons celery seed
3	Tablespoons mustard seed
1	quart vinegar
⅓	cup salt
1	Tablespoon turmeric
1	cup sugar
2	cups honey
1	cup dark corn syrup

Scrape corn from cobs. Cook until done. Chop remaining vegetables or put through food chopper. Add remaining ingredients. Cook until thick, 1 to 1½ hours. Turn into hot, sterilized jars filling to within ½ inch from top. Seal at once.
Makes 4 quarts.

India Relish

12	large green tomatoes
1	red pepper
1	green pepper
4	large onions
1	Tablespoon salt
1	cup dark honey
1	Tablespoon mustard seed
1	Tablespoon celery seed

Chop tomatoes, onions, and peppers coarsely. Drain well. Add remaining ingredients and mix thoroughly. Cook slowly until vegetables are tender and mixture is thick, about 20 minutes. Turn into hot, sterilized jars, filling to ½-inch from top. Seal at once.
Makes 3 pints.

Mild Honey Mustard

½ cup dry mustard, preferably Dijon
⅓ cup mustard seeds
⅔ cup water
¾ cup white wine vinegar
3 Tablespoons honey
2 teaspoons salt
2 teaspoons leaf tarragon, crumbled

Combine mustard, mustard seeds, and water in an electric blender; whirl until mixture is coarsely pureed. Transfer to a bowl; cover; let stand 8 hours. Stir in vinegar, honey and salt; mix well. For a creamier consistency, whirl again in electric blender. Stir in tarragon. Store in tightly covered jars in refrigerator up to several months.

Good Sauce for Steak

½ cup sour cream
2 Tablespoons prepared horseradish, drained
1 Tablespoon lemon juice
1 Tablespoon honey
2 teaspoons freeze-dried chives

Combine ingredients; blend well. Cover and refrigerate 3 to 4 hours to blend flavors.
Makes ⅔ cup.

Honey Lemon Jelly

    2½   *cups honey*
    ¾   *cup strained lemon juice*
    ½   *cup liquid fruit pectin*

Blend honey and lemon juice in large saucepan. Bring to a full, rolling boil and add pectin, stirring constantly. Heat to a full boil. Boil 1 minute. When jelly flakes from mixing spoon, remove from heat. Skim and pour into hot sterilized glasses. Cover with paraffin. Delicious with hot biscuits as well as meats.

Honey Orange Butter

    2   *Tablespoons honey*
    ½   *cup softened butter*
    2   *Tablespoons frozen concentrated orange juice*

Add honey to butter, beating until light and fluffy. Continue beating while slowly adding juice. Excellent on pancakes, waffles, French toast or toasted English muffins.
Makes ¾ cup.

Pancake and Waffle Sauce

    1   *cup Orange Blossom honey*
    ½   *cup light cream*
    2   *Tablespoons butter*
    2   *Tablespoons Grand Marnier*

Combine. Cook over low heat for 10 minutes. Pour into a preheated pitcher and serve over waffles.

Cakes, Pies & Cookies

When baking with cake mixes, always use 2 Tablespoons of honey in your favorite mix. Add the honey in a fine stream as you beat the batter. This will make for a moister cake and one that keeps well.

Lemon Honey Cake

- ½ cup shortening
- ½ cup butter
- ¾ cup sugar
- ¼ cup honey
- 5 eggs, separated
- 2 Tablespoons lemon juice
- 2 teaspoons lemon rind
- ¼ teaspoon vanilla
- 2¼ cups sifted flour
- ¾ teaspoon baking powder
- 1 teaspoon mace
- ¼ teaspoon salt

Cream shortenings and sugar thoroughly. Add honey and beat well. Add egg yolks, lemon juice and rind, and vanilla, beat thoroughly. Fold in stiffly beaten egg whites, then sifted dry ingredients. Bake in 5½x9½-inch loaf pan, lined with waxed paper, at 325° for 75 minutes.

White Cake

1 cup sugar
6 Tablespoons light-colored honey
½ cup shortening
1 teaspoon salt
½ cup egg whites (about 4)
2½ cups sifted cake flour
4½ teaspoons baking powder
⅓ teaspoon cream of tartar
¾ cup milk
1 teaspoon almond flavor

    Beat together sugar, honey, shortening, salt and ¼ cup egg whites at low speed for 5 minutes in electric mixer. Sift dry ingredients together and add. Combine milk, almond flavor, and remaining ¼ cup egg whites, and add over 3-minute period. Continue beating 2 minutes at low speed.
    Bake in two greased, 8" or 9" round cake pans lined on the bottom with waxed paper. Bake at 350⁰ degrees for 30 minutes. Cool and frost with favorite icing.

Lou McClure Willimon's Poppy Seed Cake

1 box buttered-pecan and date bits cake mix
1 box toasted coconut instant pudding-pie filling
4 eggs
½ cup vegetable oil
1 cup hot water
¼ cup poppy seeds
2 Tablespoons honey

    Preheat oven to 325⁰. Grease and flour a bundt pan, or a pan that holds a like amount of batter. Combine and mix above ingredients, and while batter is being mixed, add in 2 tablespoons honey.
    Bake in preheated oven for 40 minutes. Cool and slice. Delicious for breakfast, tea, or dessert.

Applesauce Cake

- ½ cup shortening
- 1¼ cups sugar
- ¼ cup honey
- 2 eggs, beaten
- 1¼ teaspoons vanilla
- 1 cup thick, unsweetened applesauce
- 2 cups sifted flour
- 1 teaspoon baking powder
- ½ teaspoon soda
- ¼ teaspoon salt
- 1½ teaspoons cinnamon
- 1 teaspoon cloves
- ¼ teaspoon allspice
- 1 cup raisins
- 1 cup chopped nuts

Thoroughly cream shortening, sugar, honey and eggs for 5 minutes at low speed. Add vanilla and applesauce, then sifted dry ingredients. Mix in raisins and nuts. Bake in greased 9-inch square pan in 350° oven 45 to 50 minutes.

Bette Hitch's Holland Honey Cake

- 3 cups flour
- 1 cup sugar
- 1 cup honey
- 1 cup milk
- 1 teaspoon baking soda
- 1 Tablespoon anise seed

Combine above ingredients and let stand for 2 hours. Liberally grease a loaf pan and cut brown paper to fit. Grease brown paper heavily and pour in batter. Bake in 325° oven for 1½ hours. Remove brown paper immediately and let cool.

Honey Fruitcake

3	ounces candied lemon peel
3	ounces candied orange peel
¼	pound preserved citron
¼	pound candied cherries
½	pound pitted dates
¼	pound walnut meats
½	pound pecan meats
½	pound candied pineapple
½	pound seedless raisins
1	cup butter (or margarine)
1	cup honey
5	eggs
1½	cups sifted all-purpose flour
½	teaspoon salt
1	teaspoon allspice
1	teaspoon baking powder
½	teaspoon ground nutmeg
¼	cup orange juice
½	cup all-purpose flour

Cut peels and citron in long thin strips. Halve cherries and dates. Cut nutmeats in quarters. Cut pineapple slices in eighths. Dredge combined fruits and nuts in ½ cup flour. Cream butter, add honey gradually, blending thoroughly. Add eggs, beating well.

Sift dry ingredients together. Add dry ingredients to creamed mixture, alternately with orange juice, beating well after each addition. Then fold in fruit.

Turn into 2 loaf pans which have been lined with brown paper and greased. Bake in slow oven (250°) for 3-3½ hours.

Makes two loaves.

Chocolate Cake

- ½ cup cake flour
- 6 Tablespoons cocoa
- 1 cup sugar
- 6 Tablespoons honey
- ½ cup plus 1 tablespoon shortening
- 1 teaspoon salt
- 2 whole eggs
- 1⅓ cups cake flour
- 2 teaspoons soda
- 1 cup milk
- ½ teaspoon vanilla
- 1 whole egg

Sift together ½ cup flour and cocoa. Blend with sugar, honey, shortening, salt and 2 whole eggs by mixing 5 minutes at slow speed. Sift together the 1⅓ cups flour and soda and add to above. Combine milk, vanilla, and whole egg, and add to above ingredients over a 2 minute period. Mix for another 2 minutes at slow speed.

Spoon into 2 round layer pans lined with waxed paper. Bake at 350° for 30 minutes or until done. Cool slightly for about 30 minutes, remove from pans. Ice as desired.

Carrot-Coconut Honey Cake

¾	cup oil, preferably coconut oil
½	cup honey
2	eggs
1	cup finely shredded carrots
½	cup freshly grated pineapple
½	teaspoon vanilla
1¼	cups plus 2 tablespoons all-purpose flour
1	teaspoon baking powder
½	teaspoon baking soda
½	teaspoon cinnamon
¼	teaspoon salt
¼	teaspoon ginger
¼	teaspoon cloves
1	cup finely grated coconut
1	cup finely chopped walnuts

Preheat oven to 350º. Grease and flour an 8x8x2-inch baking pan; set aside. Beat oil and honey together in a medium bowl until opaque. Add eggs, one at a time, beating well after each addition. Stir in carrots, pineapple, and vanilla.

Sift dry ingredients together 3 times. Blend into batter, beating well. Stir in nuts and coconut. Spread evenly into prepared pan and bake in oven for 45-55 minutes, or until top is nicely browned and a cake-tester inserted in the center comes out clean.

Cool completely on a wire rack before frosting with Cream Cheese Frosting or serving plain.

Cream Cheese Frosting

8	ounces cream cheese
3	Tablespoons honey
½	teaspoon vanilla

Beat all ingredients together until smooth. Spread over cooled carrot cake. Double recipe for larger cake.

Harvest Pumpkin Pie

- 1   9-inch pastry shell, unbaked
- 1   cup honey
- 1   cup sour cream
- 1½ cups cooked or canned pumpkin
- 2   teaspoons pumpkin pie spice
- ½   teaspoon salt
- 1   Tablespoon corn starch
- 3   eggs, slightly beaten
- ½   cup coarsely chopped nuts (pecan or walnut)

In a large bowl, blend honey, sour cream, pumpkin, spice, salt and corn starch with electric mixer until smooth. Fold in eggs. Turn into pastry shell. Sprinkle nuts over top. Bake at 400° for 45 minutes or until knife inserted near center comes out clean.

Pecan Pie

- ½   cup sugar
- ¾   cup light corn syrup
- 2   Tablespoons honey
- 3   eggs, slightly beaten
- 1   teaspoon vanilla
- ½   teaspoon salt
- 1½ cups pecan meats
  whipped cream for topping if desired
- 1   9-inch pastry shell

Mix ingredients, reserving half the nuts. Pour into pie shell, top with remaining nuts. Bake at 350° for 40-50 minutes.

Fudge Brownies

½	cup butter or margarine
2	1-ounce squares unsweetened chocolate
½	teaspoon salt
1	teaspoon vanilla
1	cup honey
½	cup unsifted flour
1	teaspoon baking powder
2	eggs
1	cup coarsely chopped nuts (pecan, walnut, etc.)

In saucepan, over low heat, melt together butter, chocolate, salt and vanilla. Mix well. Remove from heat. Blend in honey, flour and baking powder. Add eggs, beat well. Add nuts. Pour into well greased 9x9x2-inch pan.

Bake at 325° for 35 minutes, or until done in center. Cool on wire rack 15 minutes before marking in 16 squares. Gently remove from pan with spatula.

Footprint Cookies

1	pound soft butter
3	beaten eggs
	juice of 1 orange
1	Tablespoon grated orange peel
1	cup honey
4½	cups flour
1	teaspoon baking soda
1	cup chopped macadamia nuts or pecans

Knead all ingredients together. Make into 1-inch balls and place on ungreased cookie sheet. Press thumb into center of each, making deep well. Fill sparingly with your favorite preserve. Bake approximately 12 minutes (they will not turn brown) at 375°. Remove from oven and sprinkle with powdered sugar.

Store in air tight container layering between foil. The flavor is best 24 hours after baking. Keep well.

Makes 8 dozen.

Peanut Butter Cookies

¼ cup margarine
½ cup peanut butter
¼ cup white sugar
¼ cup brown sugar
½ cup honey
1 egg
½ teaspoon vanilla
1¼ cups sifted flour
½ teaspoon baking powder
¾ teaspoon soda
¼ teaspoon salt

Cream margarine, peanut butter, and sugars thoroughly. Add honey and beat well. Add egg and vanilla and mix. Sift together the dry ingredients and stir into creamed mixture. Form into balls and place 3-inches apart on greased cookie sheet. Flatten with flour-dipped fork or with bottom of glass dipped in flour. Bake 10 to 12 minutes in 375º oven.
Makes 4 dozen.

Milk and Honey Cookies

5 Tablespoons peanut butter
5 Tablespoons honey
10 Tablespoons powdered milk

Mix all ingredients well. This will make a stiff batter. Form into balls and roll in powdered sugar. No baking needed.

Honey-Oatmeal Bars

- ½ cup shortening
- ½ cup honey
- ½ cup brown sugar, packed
- 1 egg, well beaten
- 1 teaspoon vanilla
- ¾ cup flour
- ½ teaspoon baking powder
- ¼ teaspoon salt
- 2 cups granola or 1 cup each of rolled oats and coconut, plus ½ cup of chopped almonds
- ½ teaspoon soda

Cream shortening, honey, and sugar until light and fluffy. Add egg and vanilla, and beat well. Sift together flour, soda, baking powder and salt; add to creamed mixture. Add granola or rolled oats, coconut and nuts.

Spread in 10x15-inch greased baking pan. Bake in 350° oven for 25-30 minutes. When cool, cut into bars about 1½x2½-inches. Dust with confectioners' sugar before serving.

Makes 36 bars.

Macadamia Honey Twist

- ¼ cup honey
- 4 Tablespoons butter
- 2 cans of "pop-open" biscuits
- 1 cup finely chopped Macadamia nuts
- 4 Tablespoons cinnamon sugar

Melt honey and butter in small saucepan. Remove. Open biscuits, and stretch/pull each one to about 6 inches long. Mix nuts and cinnamon sugar together in saucer. Dip stretched biscuits in honey-butter mixture and roll in sugar, nut mixture. Twist, crescent style, and place evenly on a large cookie sheet. Bake at 400° for ten minutes.

Makes 20.

Lebkuchen
"traditional German Christmas honey cakes"

½ cup honey
½ cup molasses
1 egg
1 Tablespoon lemon juice
¾ cup brown sugar (packed)
1 teaspoon grated lemon rind
2¾ cups sifted flour
½ teaspoon soda
1 teaspoon cinnamon
1 teaspoon cloves
1 teaspoon allspice
1 teaspoon nutmeg
⅓ cup cut-up citron
⅓ cup chopped nuts

Mix honey and molasses and bring to boil. Remove from heat and cool thoroughly. Stir in egg, sugar, lemon juice and rind. Sift dry ingredients together and add to mixture, stirring well. Finally, mix in citron and nuts.

Chill dough overnight. Roll small amount at a time, keeping rest chilled. Roll out ¼-inch thick and cut into oblongs, 1½x2½-inches. Place 1-inch apart on greased baking sheet. Bake in 400° oven for 10 to 12 minutes. Bake until, when touched lightly, no imprint remains.

While cookies bake, make Glazing Icing (below). Brush it over cookies the minute they are out of oven. Then quickly remove from baking sheet. Cool and store to mellow.

Makes about 6 dozen.

Glazing Icing for Lebkuchen

1 cup sugar
½ cup water
¼ cup confectioner's sugar

Boil together sugar and water until first indication of a thread appears (230°). Remove from heat. Stir in confectioner's sugar and brush hot icing thinly over cookies. (When icing gets sugary, reheat slightly, adding a little water until clear again).

Other Good Things

Baked Bananas in Honey-Lemon Sauce

    6   ripe, firm bananas
   ¼   cup honey
    3   Tablespoons butter
    2   Tablespoons lemon juice
   ¼   teaspoon salt
   ¼   cup chopped macadamia nuts

Peel bananas and slice each in half, lengthwise. Combine remaining ingredients in a small pan and cook over low heat, stirring until butter is melted and sauce is smooth. (Can leave nuts to put on top before baking.) Place banana halves in a shallow, oven-proof dish; top with sauce and nuts and bake in 300° oven until bubbly and golden brown. Serve warm, flamed with a little brandy, if desired.
Serves 6.

Chocolate Almond Sauce

    4   squares bitter chocolate
    1   Tablespoon Cointreau
    ⅛   teaspoon salt
    ⅓   cup honey, liquid
    ⅓   cup shredded toasted almonds

In double boiler, melt chocolate with Cointreau and stir until smooth. Add salt and honey. Continue cooking over hot water until mixture is thoroughly blended. Then stir in almonds. Cover. Remove from fire and allow sauce to steam for 15 minutes, stirring occasionally. Serve lukewarm.

Chocolate Fudge Icing

    1¾   cups powdered sugar
    ¾   cup cocoa
    ¼   teaspoon salt
    3   Tablespoons butter
    1½   Tablespoons honey
    1   egg white
    2-3 Tablespoons hot milk

Sift dry ingredients together. Mix in warm bowl with remaining ingredients, except milk, until free of lumps. Add hot milk and mix until smooth. Keep in warm bowl (115°) until used, stirring occasionally. Too high a temperature causes icing to lose its shine.

Honey Ice Cream

    1   *quart milk*
    1   *quart heavy cream*
  1¾   *cups mild-flavored honey*
    1   *Tablespoon vanilla*
    6   *eggs, separated*

In saucepan, combine milk, cream and honey. Heat to lukewarm. Stir in vanilla. Chill. Beat egg whites until stiff. Using same beater, beat egg yolks until thick. Carefully blend yolks and whites. Fold into chilled mixture. Pour into chilled freezer container. Add enough milk to fill container to two-thirds capacity. Cover tightly. Set in freezer tub. Follow manufacturer's directions for correct amounts of crushed ice and salt. When frozen, remove dasher. Pack down ice cream. Replace cover. Return to freezer tub container. Set in ice and salt until ready to serve.

Variation: For Chocolate ice cream, melt 2 cups chocolate pieces completely in warm milk and cream combined.

Makes 1 gallon.

Fruit Roll Ups

  1   *cup blended fruit*
  1   *Tablespoon honey*

Use a flat cookie sheet completely covered with plastic wrap—not waxed paper. Pour fruit and honey mixture onto pan and set it in direct sun. This will take 1-2 days. When you can pull the fruit from the wrap, your fruit leather is done. Then roll it, plastic wrap and all, into a roll. Store in refrigerator or freezer.

Bob Jennings
Cream Cheese and Honey Crepes

    3   8-ounce packages cream cheese
    ¾   cup honey
    ¾   cup sugar
    1-2 Tablespoons vanilla
    1½ ounces Brandy
    1½ ounces Myers or Grand Marnier
    1   Tablespoon lemon juice
    1   Tablespoon lemon peel
    1   cup sour cream

Blend all together and spread liberally on crepes. Roll up and serve. Delicious!
Fills 25-30 7-inch crepes.

Honey Taffy

    2   cups honey
    2   cups sugar
    ⅔   cup cold water
    ⅛   teaspoon salt
    2   Tablespoons vinegar

Boil honey, sugar, and water to hard ball stage (258°). Add salt. Put in buttered dish to cool. Pull until white.

Strawberry Smoothie

    2   cups fresh strawberries, mashed
    2   cups milk
    ¼   cup honey
    1   pint vanilla ice cream

Mix and blend all ingredients until creamy smooth. Serve in 6 chilled glasses.

Honey Chocolate Sauce

    1   *6-ounce package semisweet chocolate bits*
    ½   *cup honey*
    ¾   *cup evaporated milk*

Melt chocolate bits in double boiler. Add honey and milk and stir until well blended. Serve warm or cold. Delicious with pound cake or puddings, milk shakes, and ice cream. Keeps indefinitely in refrigerator.

Party Eggnog

    12   *egg yolks*
    12   *Tablespoons honey*
    4-6   *cups dark rum, brandy, bourbon or rye*
    2   *quarts whipping cream*
    8-12   *egg whites*
        nutmeg, freshly grated

    Beat egg yolks until light in color. Beat in honey gradually. Add very slowly 2 cups of the liquor chosen, beating constantly. Let mixture stand covered for 1 hour to dispel "eggy" taste.
    Beating constantly, add 2-4 cups of liquor and 2 quarts of whipping cream. Refrigerate covered for 3 hours.
    Beat egg whites until stiff, but not dry. Fold them lightly into other ingredients. Serve sprinkled with nutmeg.
    Some people like to add a little more spirit to the recipe, remembering Mark Twain's observation that "too much of anything is bad, but too much whiskey is just enough."
    Variation: When you add the second quantity of liquor, also add 1 cup of peach brandy.